Webb's Weave of Words

Sierrah Webb

BookLeaf Publishing

Presentation by *BookLeaf Publishing*

Web: www.bookleafpub.com

E-mail: info@bookleafpub.com

ISBN: 9789395950077

First edition 2023

DEDICATION

To Zachary Louis, Natalie Elise, and Axton
Slade - my Munchkins who keep me going!

Special thanks to my hubby Josh - to whom I've
finally properly thanked for his dedication and
love. For whom I could not do this without.

To my friend Louis - Thanks for the memories
and the opportunities for growth!

A Bee Like Me

Drone took a look around the meadow. A colorful field of black and yellow sunflowers was just ahead. It was here that he would earn a great title and see the Queen. At the sunflowers, he started to work, carrying the heavy pollen to the hive over and over and over again. He got so tired, so quickly, and never had time for anything fun. "GAAAH!! No time for me! No time for play! I just cannot live this way!" So away he went, to find a field that was just right for a little bee who wanted to play.

Writing a Poem

It's not so hard to write a poem.
Seeing one, I get inspired.
I do all that's required.
It's not so hard to write a poem.

It's hard to write a poem.
What should I write?
As hard as I might,
It's hard to write a poem.

Did I just write a poem?
One that makes sense.
Why was I so tense?
I did just write a poem.

Into the Aether

Beyond the Aether, the formless in-between,
Where spirits dwell, rarely seen.
They flitter in to and fro,
And upon the aurora they brightly glow.
Although our world may seem mundane
With stretching concrete across the plane,
Into the Aether you may fly
If only you open your mind's eye.
Then, you too can dwell with those in-between.
If only for moments within a dream.

His Embrace

Pleasant Aroma.
In his warmth, I nestle in,
Vibrations welcomed.

A Girl Like Me

She took a look around the room. A colorful pile of clothes was just ahead. It was here that she would finally get to cleaning, folding, and putting away that accursed laundry. Her procrastinating was getting the best of her, but today would be the day she listened to that voice in her head. Carrying the heavy basket to and from the machines, over and over and over again, made her feel like the task would never end. She got so tired and didn't have time for anything fun. "Ugh!! Why am I like this! Why do I wait? I just cannot live this way!" So away she went, to find a solution that was just right for a girl who wanted to nothing to do with laundry day.

Flooded

Beyond the shifting sands of Thebes,
People fell upon their knees.
Unto Ra they cried and prayed
To dry upon the cascade.
But upon deaf ears their wails felled,
For this was not to be dispelled.
And into history long forgotten
Those poor fools the misbegotten.

Toxic Rain

What can you do with a rain with no water,
the kind that just falls from the sky.
No fuel for the plants, no hydration for self,
That comes in abundance and fails to provide.
It hurts to the touch, it devours all good,
Leaving only evil in its wake.
What can you do with a rain with no water,
when you can take all that, you can take.

Money Shot

In the jungle there lived a monkey,
Whose favorite game was being spunky.
Picked a fight with a gorilla
who was no match for dear Priscilla.
After one slap
he limped back,
isn't that kind of funky?

In Unseen Places

In time I've collected a thing or two,
the odds and ends of old and new.
Some would say I hoard this stuff,
but I can't seem to get enough.
The potential for greatness lies within,
a story exploited and used again.
Nick-nacks and bobbles, treasures agleam,
scavenging and hunting in places unseen.

In Admiration

Within your silhouette,
Lies features I cannot forget.
Every curve, and golden briar
Sparks within me, a burning desire.
Though I have long explored your lands
And finger-traced them, heart in hands.
I do not think I'll ever tire
Of resting within your exalted spire.

Bitter Frost

Cold wind blows northward,
In through the frigid freljord,
Onto windswept plains.

From my Love, His Heart so True

The tide rolls into the sand, as we stand hand in
hand.
We gaze upon tumultuous deluge; in my heart
you may find refuge.
As the waves come to crest, I will hold you
tightly to my chest.
With the final crashing crescendo, with you I
will gladly go
To the next sea of existence, my love for you
beyond persistence.

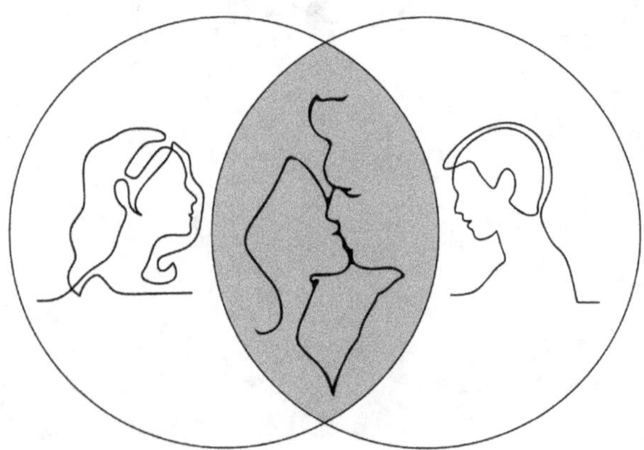

To my Love, My Heart is Too

Lost and forgotten, a torn bride.
A promised future was cast aside.
Buried deep beneath the sand.
No longer had the strength to stand.
Your shovel pierced and tore the knoll,
the persistence and patience made a hole.
Love was born from the dig,
provided me with courage to swig.
I would be yours as you chose to be mine.
Engaged before a valentine.
A victory in your history, a guidance to your all,
once forgotten and cold, I am proud and tall.
If not for your love, devotion, loyalty, and
charm,
I may still be rotting and causing self-harm.
Embracing our life has been a great bliss,
I've been grateful to you from our very first kiss.
I may take more words to express how I feel,
to be true to you is to be truly real.
I'll go with you anywhere, as far as you'd travel,
through ocean or jungle, on mud or on gravel.
May long lasting peace reign in our existence.
No matter the location, no matter the distance.
My heart is yours and so you'll have me

with you by my side, I am truly happy.

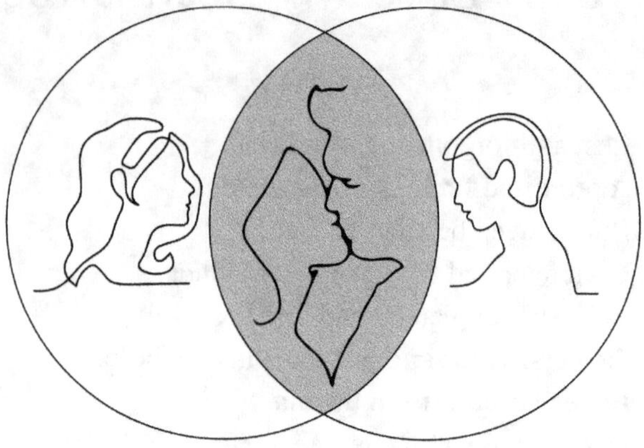

Your Eyes

Rainbows vibrance coalesce,
Shifting now upon the essence.
And while they often shine bright,
They too can be the greyest sight.
I reach out now beyond the veil,
The fog passes without fail.
That rainbow again will be mine,
When it's opalescent colors brightly shine.

So You want to be a Grown Up

So you want to be a grown-up.
That's what I used to say,
I'll show you what it's really like,
to grow and be this way.

I have a job and drive a car,
a pet and kiddos three,
a husband that I love so much.
A growing family.

A space that's mine to rest my head,
some hobbies that I love.
The food I crave is here for me.
My life fits like a glove.

The catch is what I'm telling you,
so, listen in real good.
The thing to know is already known.
It's easily understood.

To have a job, and have a car,
you have to have the means.
To get the means, you gotta learn,
and learning's in your teens.

To have a space that's all your own
with all your favorite things.
You have to take it step by step,
and that's what childhood brings.

To find your love and settle down
takes lots of work inside.
Bring peace into your heart and then
reflect on being kind.

The perks of being grown are nice,
but really what has changed?
To be the future self you see
is mindset rearranged.

Just a Park Bench

Could you Imagine,
Someone, out in the world
at this very moment,
can look at a park bench
and see it only as a place to rest.
It's easy, isn't it. To see things as they are meant
to be.

Could you Imagine, Harder now.
Someone, out in the world
at this very moment
can look at a park bench
and see it as a memory, a memorial even.
Even then, we print these for the eyes to see.

Could you Imagine, hardest of all.
Someone, out in the world
at this very moment
can look at a park bench
and see that it is the portal of wonder to new
horizons,
a place to be close to nature, or a place to touch
the clouds.

Could you imagine, Just for a little while,
That you are that someone,
stretching your imagination
soaking in all that is wonderful,
all from the comfort of a park bench.

Eldritch

Quakes and shadows from the deep
with trepidation, a cautious peep.
From worlds unknown, of terrible wonders,
Yearning release, the Eldritch thunders.
In sight of this abominable end,
the fate of the cosmos I must defend.
Mechanical gears are strictly guarded.
To release the beast would be worlds departed.

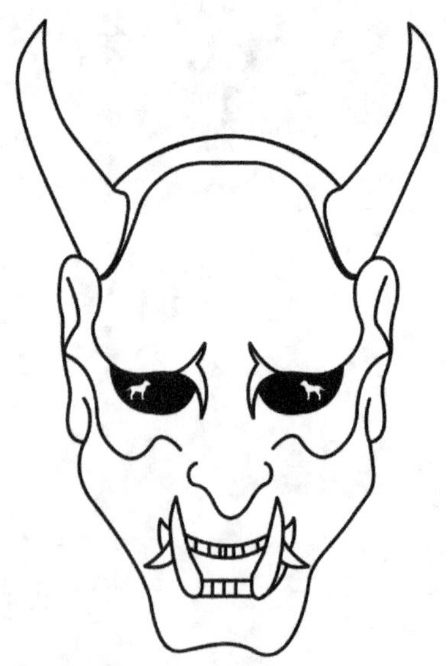

Sleep Paralysis

My soul is full of longing,
my body keeps me here.
I feel it coming out of me,
I manage just a tear.

I lie here paralyzed.
Eager as I try
to move, to yell, to make it known
that I am still alive.

I slow my breathing just a bit
to keep from burning out.
Exhausted from the wasted time,
I tried to scream and shout.

I get to see the demons now,
so patiently they wait,
to take me from the wretched world
succumbing to my fate.

Slowly after fighting hard,
my soul decides to rest.
Fitting back into my self
I'm automatically stressed.

I bolt up like I've been revived
my racing heart is pumping.
Anxiety is coursing through me,
my mind is quickly jumping.

The fit I threw was real, its true
but no one here can see.
Cursed to feel the soul of longing
desperate of leaving me.

For the Love of Pets

Blue sparkling eyes,
White lush tail, Canine slumbers.
But why do you smell...

Keeping a Secret

I have a little secret,
a juicy little thing.
It jumps and turns and spins about
it makes me want to sing!

It's like a jumping bean,
a toddler on the run,
a boiling water molecule,
a doggy having fun.

I got to hold it in!
the waiting is the worst.
The secret grew in size and shape.
I think I'm gonna burst!

I told the little secret
to its originator.
It means I kept the secret
and I feel a whole lot greater.

Opportunity for Reflection

In times like these we come to wonder,
Of choices made, success and blunder.
The need for answers, most of all,
When we rise and when we fall.
Who can we thank for our success?
What has given us so much stress?
Where can we say it all went wrong?
What did I learn to get so strong?
In times like these, we ask inside,
Is it shame or is it pride?
To walk this road that's lead me here,
A life of courage a life of fear.
But alas, a light, that guides me now,
presents to me a print, a how,
A way to get my story read,
A chance to spill words from my head.

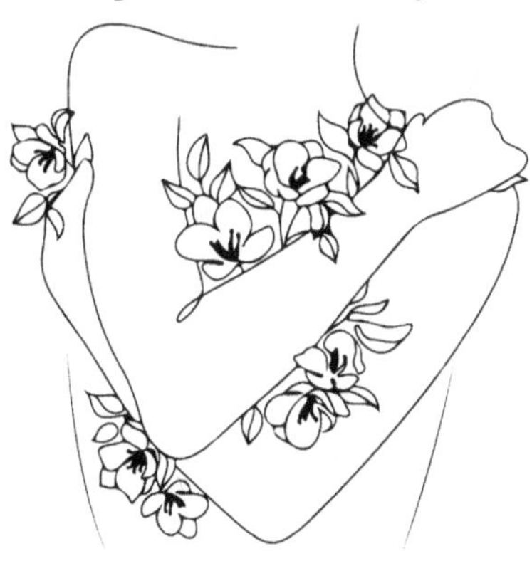